This One Life

poems by

Lee Robinson

Finishing Line Press
Georgetown, Kentucky

This One Life

for Fitz and Salley

ACKNOWLEDGMENTS

"A Sandwich, Like a Prayer" was published in *Comstock Review*
"Heaven" was published in *Tar River Poetry*
"Winter" was published in the anthology, *Senior Class*, Lamar University
Press

Publisher: Leah Huete de Maines
Editor: Christen Kincaid
Cover Art: Ann Mcaden
Author Photo: Lee Robinson
Cover Design: Elizabeth Maines McCleavy

Order online: www.finishinglinepress.com
         also available on amazon.com

Author inquiries and mail orders:
Finishing Line Press
PO Box 1626
Georgetown, Kentucky 40324
USA

Contents

This One Life 1

A Sandwich, Like a Prayer 5

The Child 7

For Laura 8

The Black Car 10

Remind Me 11

Providence 12

Heaven 14

Scat 16

We Send Them Off 17

Had I Known 18

Shared Witness 19

The Web 21

After the Flood 22

Winter 24

Wild Turkeys 26

Axis 27

Unpacking 28

What the Light Says 29

Learning to Love My Armadillo 33

This One Life

How bizarre to be born at all and stranger still
the cosmic roulette that propels the little ball
of you into a year, a month, a day, a spot
on the globe, a tribe. For me, it was 1948,

Charlotte, North Carolina, parents pinching pennies
but rich in the family lore of aristocracy—
lost plantations, lost fortunes in cotton—
mostly myth, but old myths not forgotten,

and so that year the Dixiecrats divorced the Democrats.
I bunkered in the womb until the doctor tore me out.
Daddy got a better job, Mama said goodbye to hers,
they saved, bought a house, a car.

Before long I had a brother. First grade, in 1954,
I walked to school, sat in my all-white classroom unaware
of *Brown v. Board of Ed*, whose all deliberate speed
didn't change a thing for the kids on the other side

of the tracks. I was an awkward girl, a stranger
in my own neighborhood but an amazed observer,
like John Glenn going round the earth in his capsule—
so much mystery outside my little porthole.

I knew almost nothing about sex when Marilyn died
in 1962. I locked my bedroom door, kept my lust inside.
Out there the trembling world held its collective breath
as Khrushchev and Kennedy traded threats.

Daddy built a basement shelter—jugs of water,
Chef Boyardee, a deck of cards, Monopoly. Mama
made me run from school to home to see if I'd survive.
I bombed, but lived to graduate, revived

by the promise of college, all-girls, but blessedly away.
On weekends, buses hauled us up the highway
to fraternity parties where (anesthetized with gin)
we let ourselves be pawed by good Virginia men.

What about women's lib, you're thinking, what about NOW?
Still shaky in my womanhood, I left for Boston, snow,
the sprawling university, my anonymity a balm. Tried
to make sense of my murderous country, mourned

Martin Luther King and Bobby Kennedy. Cities burned
and there were riots in my brain. I stood outside
the White House screaming *Hey Hey LBJ, how many kids
did you kill today?* 1969, the year I was married—

still half-girl—I wore a white dress, my grandmother's veil,
and on my father's arm walked down the aisle.
Just months before, I'd made love the first time
(we didn't say screwed) while men invaded the moon.

I was halfway through law school when I had my first child.
What was I thinking? With his mouth at my breast I crammed
for Criminal Law. I'm a woman now, *I can do it all,*
I passed the bar and Saigon fell.

I couldn't afford to fail, one of five "lady lawyers"
in Charleston, 1975. I wore high heels and pantyhose
and a tight little smile. I was smart. I was tough.
My skirts were short. *May it please the court.*

The year of my daughter's birth, 1978, the daredevil
Wallenda fell from a tight-rope strung between hotels.
I balanced between work and home—in one hand a pacifier,
a briefcase in the other. Days toppled into months, years,

until my husband left and everything exploded:
Khobar Towers, Olympic Park, Flight 800,
my heart. When the dust settled I looked around
and found, alone in my house, I was more at home.

I fell in love and married again—roulette, a lucky win.
I left the law. Peace at last, I thought, but one morning
in 2001 as I worked on a poem my husband called:
Turn the TV on. Now. I watched over and over, hypnotized,

to make myself believe the Towers were gone. My daughter
trembled on the deck of *The Intrepid*, blocks from disaster—
her first job out of college, raising money for a museum
to our military might. My expat son called from London,

suddenly all-American. We went to war in shock and awe.
In '08 I turned 60, the market crashed, bleakness until Obama.
I let myself believe we might begin again with *Yes we can*
but in the year my grandson was born a white man

walked into Mother Emanuel. They welcomed him.
He waited until they bowed their heads to bring out his gun.
Afterward the Dixie flag came down and hate hid underground
for an instant until *Make America Great Again*.

Now I am 77. I live seven miles from a tiny Texas town
you've never heard of, down a county road, Old No. 9,
then up the dirt road to the house at the top of the hill.
(If you cross the creek you've gone too far.) If you come, call

first. Most days I keep to myself, except for the old man
who tolerates my rants. We have our poetry, our land.
There are rattlesnakes here, so I wear boots, a wide-brimmed hat
to keep the sun off though the doctor says it's too late for that.

Where do we come from? Who are we? How I got here
I'm not quite sure. Where are we going? Every year the summer's
hotter. My old home in Charleston drowns a little more.
I'm mired in time but losing it: so much I don't remember

yet more I regret, so much to be amazed by, less I understand.
I see darkly, through thick prisms. I wring my wrinkled hands
but still I sometimes clap and sing. I grind my teeth
and practice gratitude for this one life, which is, I tell myself,

enough. When Death comes knocking, surely
I should open the door and let her in, but more likely
I'll keep the latch on, peer through the crack
and beg for another year: *Not yet*, I'll say, *Not yet*.

A Sandwich, Like a Prayer

In my eighth decade I am making amends
for the seven before. (Maybe the first shouldn't count,
I was just a child.) It's my penance, this sandwich,
because near the end of my nineteenth year I erred.

You, reading this, might say it wasn't so terrible,
she was still half-child, it was the late sixties,
she'd just discovered women's lib, surely this was just
her way of saying to her mother *I will not be like you,*

I will not cater to him. Maybe, you might think,
she went a little too far, still, it was no sin.
But this is not about me only. It never is.
There were the father and the mother. My father

(I did not know this then) who at eight came home
from school to find his father dead, a gunshot
to the head, and my mother whose father
carried on with the company secretary—*flagrantly,*

as they said back then, until his wife took to drink.
No one told me any of this until I was thirty.
Is that an excuse? I'd come home from college for a week,
Christmas or spring break, I don't remember,

but only the feeling of being caged again.
My mother went out for a while and left me
with my father. He was not yet an invalid. "At noon
he'll want his sandwich," she said, then told me how

to make it. Just so. "On toasted bread. One slice
of bologna, one slice of cheese. Not too much mayonnaise."
I rose up in my righteousness: "Why can't he make his own
damn sandwich?" The words, and how I said them, like a knife.

The sharpness, the thrill. But then her face, that look,
as if she knew—of course she knew—but could not say,
I understand. She left. I made his sandwich. He ate, though not
with any appetite. We didn't speak. His eyes were watery,

that rheumy blue that saw things far away but missed
the nearer truths. My eyes are green, yet so like his. My hands
like hers. And so this sandwich, for you, a man he never met.
Forgive me for all I do not understand. Forgive us all

for what we do not know, for what we know
but cannot say. Take, eat. Such a simple
thing, made the way you like it:
a sandwich, like a prayer.

The Child

The child opened the door and walked into the yard.
She'd been there a thousand times before
but this was different. Now it was all new, the sun
sparking every tree and bush, the dew quivering

on each blade of grass. Maybe, she thought, this
is the first morning I am really *myself*.
Of this feeling she would say nothing to her mother, inside
chatting with the neighbor, nor to her father

who would come home after sundown, too tired to talk.
She wanted to say hello to everything, to introduce herself
to her own backyard, but also to say goodbye, as if
she might never come here again.

She kneeled, sucked the stem of the dark pink flower,
understood how the world could be both sweet and sour.
She stirred the dirt with a stick and tasted it,
braided the fallen needles of the pine into a bracelet.

She lay down in the grass and felt each blade. She slept.
Later, over supper, she said nothing of how deep and sweet
that sleep was, nor how, so awake now, she could see them all—
herself, her family—as if from afar, for what they were.

For Laura

which was the only name I knew for you.
Am I audacious or just plain crazy to hope
this poem might find its way to you?
If you're still alive you're in your nineties.
You came to us weekdays, some Saturdays,
to cook and clean and—as my mother said—mind
the children. You used the toilet
on our back porch. Two or three times
I ventured there in secret, to sit where you sat—
in winter, the seat so cold it shocked like a slap,
in summer the sun leered through the slats
of the swinging door.

You came on the bus, in your uniform, blue
with white at the collar and cuffs, starched
and pressed. Sometimes I'd pretend to be sick, stay
home from school so we could watch the soaps together
while you did the ironing. I asked a hundred questions.
You ironed and answered, explained the stories.
It's a hard thing sometimes, you said. *Love. But don't you
worry about it, honey. Plenty of time for that.*
Once I asked if you had a boyfriend. You made a face, part
frown, part smile, which meant
Mind your own business.

What made me ask, one Saturday, *Can I go home with you?*
I was six, shy. What made you say *Yes* when
everything about our worlds said *No?*
This was 1954, Charlotte, North Carolina.
I begged my parents to let me go. We rode the bus together
to a part of town I'd never seen before.

I remember the house. Small, full of voices:
your parents, aunts and uncles, cousins.
A girl about my age ran her fingers
down the length of my pigtails.
I touched her curls, felt the shiver in her giggle.

Hot dogs on a grill in the backyard. The yard
swept clean, red roses along the fence.
Potato salad, lemonade, a chocolate cake
with inch-thick icing.

Go ahead, you said,
have a second helping. Careful laughter,
all of us on our best behavior
until my father came to take me home.

The Black Car

I have seen myself in the '57 yellow Chevrolet with the plastic
    daisy on the antenna—
my father's idea, so I could find my car in the high school
    parking lot.
I have seen myself in the green bug on my first wedding day, red
    bows on the doors,
tin cans tied behind. Seen myself in the Olds station wagon, that
    bronze goliathan
that hauled the kids and dogs, the groceries and footlockers.
    Seen myself
in the scarlet convertible I thought might make me young again,
    which I sold
because at the end of a workday I could hardly crawl out of it,
    sold it for the gray
Toyota, more suitable for middle age. After that there's an
    automotive blur, a few more
cars disappearing in the rearview mirror like exhaust, or
    exhaustion, until I see myself—
fast forward—in the black car, my little jar of dust in the back
    seat, riding towards oblivion.

Remind Me

There was the time our loving drove the bed across the floor,
the marks of its travel on old heart pine still there
twenty years later. We talk about refinishing but procrastinate,
perhaps not wanting to lose such luscious evidence.
There was the time we walked along the narrow road
in North Carolina, above us the steep hill, below
the drop-off to the churning creek. Every now and then
a car or truck would come too fast around the bend and
send us scampering into brush, but mostly the road seemed
all ours, the few houses quiet, not a human soul around,
just a cow or two, and when we came to the pasture
that covered the hill with its soft green pleasure
we couldn't resist. We rolled in it, our bodies
unaware of anything beyond our lust, beyond our bliss.
There was the time on the Texas coast, up early for birding—
the throngs of ducks, the elegance of egrets and ibises wading
in shallow water, the little blue heron an otherworldly color,
electric indigo—all of it, water and sky, birds and water,
intoxicating. You turned the car off the deserted road
and in the back seat we made love, madly, made
ourselves come to our animal senses, bend to our human
need. There were other times as good, times stolen,
it seemed, from time itself. Love, can you remember
more? Remind me, then, as we lie together in our
seventies, different bodies but the same old need, the same
desire now tinged with fear, knowing the loss to come.

Providence

"You need to come back to the hospital now,"
says the nurse on the telephone. She's trained
not to say more. "Just come."
I've been away an hour—
quick dinner, glass of wine—
a respite from the five-day vigil,
but when I walk into my mother's room
I'm a guilty child again:
I've let her die alone.

She lies on her back, eyes closed,
mouth open as if to shout against the silence.
A doctor—not hers, just one
whose turn it is to do such things—
bends down to listen with a stethoscope,
scribbles something on the chart,
says she's sorry, hurries out.

Then comes the chaplain
trussed in his shiny suit:
Bob Perry, Providence,
says the pin on his lapel.
How crass, I think, to advertise
like this, as if he holds the only key
to the hereafter, but then I remember
where we are: Providence Hospital,
Columbia, South Carolina, the town
I once called home.

"Let us pray," he says, reaching
for my hand, and I mouth
the words I've almost forgotten.
Thy kingdom come. Thy will be done.

My mother in late life
prayed daily, perhaps to seek forgiveness
for her sins, more likely
just to ease her loneliness,
and though her God seldom answered
she kept talking
as she'd been taught to do
in even the most difficult conversations.

Before she ceased to speak she turned to me,
squeezed my hand so hard it hurt and cried,
"Please pray for me."

Is this the answer she waited for,
this most unlikely providence,
her will be done,
her non-believing daughter
standing by her bed
holding the preacher's hand?

For her, I bow my head.

Heaven

Admit it,
you liked the idea—
no worms, no rot,

being barefoot
forever on cloud-soft
streets. Admit

you yearned
for weightlessness,
ridding yourself

of that old backpack
stuffed with sins.
About the reunions

you weren't so sure
but you couldn't refuse
without seeming unangelic,

so every day now
you meet an old friend or two,
and you talk about—what else?—

what brought you here:
the heart attack, the stroke,
the truck without its brakes.

If you change the subject to, say,
happiness, you risk being a bore:
Nobody talks about joy anymore.

What disappoints the most?
These wings. Admit
you craved a pair of your own,

imagining the rush of air
under them, the gliding, the soaring,
the great long swoop of the sky.

Why is it now
you hate the sight of them?
Why is it you miss the earth

so much—stones underfoot,
the worm in the dirt, the smell,
after rain, of morning?

Your only heaven now
is sleep, the sweet slow
dream of falling.

Scat

Late August in Texas, at ten a.m. already
over ninety, and here it is again on the walkway
to our front door, your calling card, this turd
already black and hard, like a sausage
left too long in the frying pan.

"It's the gray fox," my husband says,
"marking its territory." I aim the hose,
wash it away, but the next morning
it's back, the same but newer crap.
"Shit," I say, shooting the hose again,

this time with more power so that the poop
is waterborne across the driveway and
into the weeds, startling a cardinal.
On the third day it's born again, and it occurs to me
the better strategy's to step over it, let you,

your spot already marked, feel victory,
maybe find some other place to claim.
After all, I've spent enough of my life
dealing with much worse shit than this.
I've seen it all, heard all its names—

feces, stool, dung, deuce, the childhood
Number Two—seen how it devises such clever
disguises, how sometimes it flies
out of human mouths, turds turned into words,
raining on crowds who clap and clap, clueless

at what they're clapping at. Compared to that
your scat is downright dear—left here without malice,
an all-natural amalgam of mice, grasshoppers, persimmons,
an occasional crawfish from the creek.
We'll let it be, step over it.

We Send Them Off

for Uvalde's children

By car or bus we send them off
to kindergarten, first grade,
with a hug and a kiss
we let them go

with backpack and lunchbox
we send them off, our children
who carry on their little backs
the invisible terrible thing

not spoken of
by us who let them go
because we dare not
name this fear: that all our love

won't keep them safe,
that love alone
is not enough
to bring them home.

Had I Known

How can we leave, it's so beautiful here,
I said before we left on the long-planned trip.
It was early May, before summer
would scorch the ranch, the best time for birds,

our fields covered with flowers:
purple verbena, red-and-yellow blanket flower,
blue sage. This was before the virus, when
we took travelling for granted, could fly

across the ocean to see grandchildren, fall
asleep in Austin and wake in London.
Don't forget it's spring there, too, you said,
and of course it was, the fields of England

lush and green, the gardens putting ours to shame.
At Kew we sat on a bench while the kids
tumbled on the grass and squealed, as if
to mark the place as theirs, rename it Pure Delight.

Had I known it would be years before
I'd see them again, I'd have hugged them longer.
I would have said, *How can we leave you?*
You're so beautiful!

Shared Witness

Come, you said, bring poems. Any theme's okay, but we
suggest healing and community, shared witness.

I know what healing means, and community. I know
how to witness and to share. But shared witness, is that
some term of art I missed along the way? I Google,
find this:

> vSAN 7 Update introduces a shared witness option
> for 2-node cluster configurations. It is cost-efficient
> in terms of physical resources, manageability, design
> and operations.

Do humans really talk like this?

Then, reading on, I come to something from a journal of applied
   psychology:
Co-witnesses Talk, A Survey of Eyewitness Discussion, how
when two people see the same thing and later discuss it, their
   memories change.
I know about that. In another life I was a lawyer.

But that's not what I'm after. I read on, more psychology, but closer to
   home,
an article that opens with Maya Angelou. *There is no greater agony*,
   she says,
than bearing an untold story inside of you.

Bearing witness, the therapist writes in language I can understand,
*is a valuable way to process an experience…to lighten our emotional
   load.*

And I think of us, here tonight, who've come to celebrate survival,
who've come through months of loss, horrors often borne alone,
death all around us, fearing for family, far from family, far, sometimes,
from our old selves, from who we thought we were.

I look out at your faces and know there's a story inside you,
    waiting to be told,
waiting to be heard, and that's what will save us, the telling, the
    listening.

This is a prosy poem, maybe not a poem at all, a rambling
clumsy thing in search of itself, like an old woman walking in a
dark house whose rooms go on forever, her hands reaching out,
trying not to fall, trying not to hit a wall, until she comes to a
familiar place and someone who loves her,

and she breathes a little easier,
as she tells, and he listens.

The Web

I wake at three, deep dark, rain
drumming the metal roof,
when thunder strikes near enough
to shake me into thinking once again

how I would do without you, how
I might live in this house alone,
get up and turn the coffee on,
set out one cup, the other just a shadow

on the kitchen counter. How would I raise
the shade, open myself to a world
without you in it? And this bird,
this one at the feeder—who might I praise

his beauty to, but you?—this woodpecker
coming for his meal of suet, so intent but unaware
we humans share this moment like a morning prayer,
unspoken, for fear he'll scare

and fly, that something in his fright might tear
the web, invisible, that holds our lives together.

After the Flood

For weeks after the flood
we stayed away from the creek, until
that afternoon our friend came out to the country
with his camera. We had lunch first, and wine,
our small talk treading in the shallows,
never going too far out or deep.
I remember how his heavy lids
almost hid his eyes
and how he laughed as he sank his spoon
into his ice cream, saying, "I guess
the drugs and the cholesterol
can fight it out."

Afterward we took the narrow path
through the high grass, watching for snakes—
it was late spring—and he talked as we walked, at ease
with himself, it seemed, and with the wildness of the place.
We stood on the limestone shelf overlooking the creek
listening to the waterfall, and after a while
my husband pointed out the spot where the old elm
had clung to the bank until
the hundred-year flood yanked it out by the roots
and splintered its great thick trunk.
We reminisced about the shade it gave in summer,
the giant umbrella of yellow in the fall.
The hole was still visible, though weeds and silt
had begun to fill it in.

Our friend didn't respond
with false comforts, didn't say Nature has her way,
a wisdom we can't fathom, or that our sadness
would fade with time. None of that nonsense.
He understood how one loss pours into another
until the heart floods over.
We stood together, arms around each other,
listening to the sound of water
running over stone.

Then he lifted his camera,
adjusted for the light. "Let's have a smile," he said,
and took the shot. We offered to take one of him
but he shook his head. Did he know
he would kill himself before the year was out?

In the photo we two survivors
hold each other, oblivious,
for that instant, of what it means
to be without.

Winter

Haven't you been lost
to yourself
looking out the window
without seeing

until the old elm
blooms with birds
its dark limbs
alive with them

and your heart stirs,
you see what the tree
has been trying to tell you
about living

Look
how it bends with the wind
who comes this day
for a little ballet

See how the waxwings
in their elegant
everyday costumes
delight it

how it doesn't waste
its precious time
craving a finer landscape
with a better view

or quarreling with death
which is no enemy
but was there in the seed
from the beginning

Haven't you been
too long looking for home
as if it were somewhere
not here, not now?

And as for happiness,
that fickle temptress,
let the old tree tell you
what you already know:

how to be alone,
how to wait
for the company of waxwings
and how to let them go.

Wild Turkeys

Emissaries from another world, these
feathered dinosaurs, they come for seeds
that fall from the feeder
at sunrise, again at dusk.
I like to watch them gather—
their long legs, their bodies
more feather than flesh, moving
with a jerky grace
but always, even in this place,
that wariness.

When I see them on my morning walk
I whisper, "Relax, we aren't
the kind who shoot." But gunshot
echoes off the limestone hills
and fear is always with them.
It's eons old, bred in the bone.
They know the law of tooth and claw,
know not to trust the creature who stands upright,
who stops to look, who lifts the thing and aims,

and so they scatter,
though I am no murderer,
and these are only binoculars.

Axis

He was there when I looked through
half-closed blinds, the young Axis buck,
only five feet away, and I could see
the stripes down his spine, black
and white, the soft caramel of his coat
spotted with white, his antlers a pair
of dancers never touching.

I kept very still. He did not see me.
He bent to graze and I watched him
take unhurried pleasure in his meal. I'd been
at my desk too long, working on a poem
that balked at its possibilities, something
about the innocent beauty of youth,
how even the plainest among us

seem to have it yet squander it, when
the buck turned and ran. I couldn't see
what startled him. I stood to stretch, felt
the abacus of my spine count the years, then
I turned back to the poem, which was so new
it could not know, not yet,
what it might become.

Unpacking

I wake this morning before my old friend
the sun, who'll come soon enough to shake me
into doing the things that must be done,

but for now there's this hour
of luscious roaming in the deep wide dark
unspoiled by should or ought,

this quiet where the petty tyrant *I*
is shushed, where old bones rise
and leave the room, go traveling.

No need for memory now. Here
the feeble brain can falter, fail and
find a sort of freedom. Mid-morning

I'm still wandering, aimless, happy,
when she calls—my friend, an invitation
to a dinner party, last-minute, tonight.

Nice people, I tell myself, and I should go,
but no, I can already hear the chattering.
Sorry, I say, I've been away,
an unplanned trip. I'm still unpacking.

What the Light Says

1.

I was five, on the sidewalk in front of my house.
Charlotte, North Carolina. Winter, 1953,
the last sunlight reaching through the trees
to speak to me:

Remember, you won't come again to this place,
this time. My play of rays is for this day only,
is yours only now, here.

Because I wanted to make it stay, I argued:
But can't I come back tomorrow and see you again?
You can be my friend.

I felt a chill as the light withdrew.
The darkness exposed my parents' lie,
that we would be together for a long, long time
and when we died we'd meet again in heaven.

I turned back towards the house, my mother
making supper, my father hanging his hat on the hook
near the back door, his eyes full of worry,
my little brother in cowboy garb, always ready
for a fight. In that house no one ever said, "I love you."

What made us a family? Some unspoken vow
that we'd go on, do what needed to be done, one foot
in front of the other. Hastily we blessed the meal:
"God is great and God is good,
let us thank him for our food."

I wanted to tell them about the light but knew
no matter what I said, my words wouldn't be right.

2.

I married the boy I'd known forever,
the boy from home. In college we stood together
at the museum, parsing Gauguin's huge painting.
D'où venons-nous? Que sommes-nous? Où allons nous?
We knew we'd have to prove ourselves somehow,
somewhere, but not yet.

I've forgotten why we moved to Michigan
but this was the early seventies and we felt obliged
to escape expected things. I typed for a professor,
sneaked poetry when time allowed. My husband got a job
as a security guard at night, kept watch over a parking garage,
got stoned to make it bearable.

We had a roommate, a guy named Walt who kept mostly
to himself, but one winter night he brought out his toboggan.
There's a great hill in the Arboretum, he said, *and plenty
of snow. The gate's locked now but I know how
to get in.* We were still young enough to believe
in the curative power of danger. We trudged in the dark,
snow falling fast, to the top of the hill. Our trespass
gave the trek an extra thrill.

I rode in the middle, my husband in front, Walt
at the rear where he could push to get us going.
I held my breath. Soon the old world opened
into something new, the darkness lit by glint of snow,
snow tracing the shapes of bare trees. Down, down we went
until a hummock sent us flying, the toboggan a giant
wingless bird. On and on it flew with a mind of its own.
I heard Walt yell but could not tell whether out of fright or joy.

At last a snowdrift slammed us to a stop.
I lay on my back looking up for stars, for something familiar.
I felt my heart beating hard and the ground around me
reverberating, an insistent hum, as if it were trying
to comfort me.

That husband is not my husband anymore
and Walt, if he's alive, would be in his eighties.
Sometimes I feel I am still on that toboggan
holding my breath.

3.

I am an old woman now living on a Texas ranch
seven miles from the nearest town.
If you ask me how I got here I will tell you a story
that makes some sense—of years, places, children,
houses, jobs, divorce, love lost and found,
but it won't answer Gauguin's questions.
Where do we come from? Who are we?
Where are we going?

I am doing my best to live without answers.
I take my lessons from the trees. There's a giant elm
not far from the house, at least a century old.
Who knows how many northers it's withstood,
how many droughts, but I doubt it worries
about tomorrow's weather. I know the elm will die
as all things must but I need it to outlast me.
I can't bear to lose another friend, another love.

At night my husband and I cling to each other
and talk about the things we don't understand anymore,
our sense that sense is slipping away, our country turned
as mean as my demented uncle who in his last days
took an axe to the heirloom grandfather clock.

Did he think he could stop time, go back
to being young again or was it that he couldn't bear
to hear the mournful *bong, bong, bong*
announce another hour?

Through the living room window
we watch the sun go down, the last rays
playing on the elm's bare limbs. I am still waiting
for the words to tell you
what the light says.

Learning to Love My Armadillo

Where do you come from,
and why to this patch of grass around my house
when just beyond, wild acres crawl with worms
and grubs, a cornucopia of ants? A neighbor says
Pour gas down the burrow but my brother,
in South Carolina, swears by his shotgun, sat up
one April night when his wife was out of town,
all night swigging coffee and scotch until he got one.
They're blind, he says, and dumb, but hard to trap.
Don't wait—they reproduce like crazy.

A friend recommends mothballs, so I give it a try,
but now when I wake at three and turn on the outside light
there's nothing but the white detritus of my foolishness
and the holes you've dug, my armadillo.
I go back to bed, can't sleep, consider abandoning
the notion of a yard, my need for order. I settle
on an attitude not quite forgiveness but at least
appreciation for your faithfulness.
I know you're out there in the dark
and soon enough I'll be under this dirt
you churn for sustenance.

Come then, my little armored one,
come claw your way into my heart.

Lee Robinson's first poetry collection, *Hearsay*, won the Poets Out Loud Prize from Fordham University Press, judged by Robert Wrigley, and the Violet Crown Award from the Writers' League of Texas. Her second collection, *Creed*, was published by Plainview Press. She has published short stories, essays and poetry in many magazines and journals, including *Harper's, The New York Times, Texas Observer, Crab Orchard Review* and *American Book Review*. She is a three-time winner of the S.C. Arts Commission's Fiction Prize for her short stories. She has also published two novels, *Lawyer for the Dog* and *Lawyer for the Cat* (Thomas Dunne Books) and a young adult novel, *Gateway* (Houghton Mifflin, starred review Publisher's Weekly). Lee has received fellowships from the National Endowment for the Humanities, the South Carolina Arts Commission and the Writers' League of Texas.

Lee grew up in the Carolinas. She practiced law in South Carolina for 25 years and served as the executive director of an 11-county legal aid program there. Lee was elected the first female president of the Charleston Bar Association. While in Charleston she taught Constitutional Law at the Citadel.

She now lives on a ranch in the Texas hill country with her husband, the physician and writer Jerry Winakur. She and Jerry have co-taught seminars at Trinity University and the University of Texas at San Antonio. At the Center for Medical Humanities and Ethics in San Antonio they designed and taught a course for medical students, Medicine through Literature. Together they received the Literary Excellence Award from Gemini Ink, San Antonio's center for readers and writers.

www.ingramcontent.com/pod-product-compliance
Lightning Source LLC
Chambersburg PA
CBHW022046080426
42734CB00009B/1265